One Direction

By Lynn Peppas

Crabtree Publishing Company

www.crabtreebooks.com

Crabtree Publishing Company

www.crabtreebooks.com

To my daughter, Sofia

Author: Lynn Peppas
Publishing plan research and development:
Sean Charlebois, Reagan Miller
Crabtree Publishing Company
Coordinating editor: Laura Durman
Editors: Kathy Middleton, Laurie Thomas
Proofreader: Shannon Welbourn
Photo researcher: Clare Hibbert
Series and cover design: Ken Wright
Layout: sprout.uk.com
**Production coordinator and
prepress technician:** Ken Wright
Print coordinators: Katherine Berti,
Margaret Amy Salter

Photographs:
Alamy: © London Entertainment: pages 1, 13;
© WENN.com/ AlamyCelebrity: page 12;
© epa european pressphoto agency b.v.: page
15; © Lebrecht Music and Arts Photo Library:
page 23
Corbis: © Tom Meinelt/Splash News: pages 5,
20, 28; © Nico Fell/Demotix: page 14; © John
A. Angelillo: page 18; © Vinspired/Splash
News: page 24; © Comic Relief/Splash News:
page 25
Getty Images: © Jo Hale/Redferns
Keystone Press: PA Photos: page 21; wenn.com:
page 22
Photoshot: © LFI: page 6; © Retna: page 16;
© Retna Pictures: page 17;
Shutterstock.com: Jaguar PS: cover;
© Featureflash: page 4; © Mr Pics: pages 7, 9,
10, 26; © Alexandra Glen/Featureflash: page 8;
© Joe Seer: page 11

Every effort has been made to trace copyright holders and to obtain their permission for use of copyright material. The authors and publishers would be pleased to rectify any error or omission in future editions. All the Internet addresses given in this book were correct at the time of going to press. The author and publishers regret any inconvenience caused if addresses have changed or sites have ceased to exist, but can accept no responsibility for any such changes.

Produced for Crabtree Publishing Company
by Discovery Books

Library and Archives Canada Cataloguing in Publication

Peppas, Lynn
One Direction / Lynn Peppas

(Superstars!)
Includes index.
Issued also in electronic formats.
ISBN 978-0-7787-1049-3 (bound).--ISBN 978-0-7787-1053-0 (pbk.)

1. One Direction (Musical group)--Juvenile literature. 2. Boy
bands--Great Britain--Biography--Juvenile literature. I. Title.
II. Series: Superstars! (St. Catharines, Ont.)

ML3930.O585P424 2013   j782.42164092'2   C2013-900432-7

Library of Congress Cataloging-in-Publication Data

Peppas, Lynn.
One Direction / by Lynn Peppas.
pages cm. -- (Superstars!)
Includes index.
ISBN 978-0-7787-1049-3 (reinforced library binding) --
ISBN 978-0-7787-1053-0 (pbk.) -- ISBN 978-1-4271-9299-8 (electronic
pdf) -- ISBN 978-1-4271-9223-3 (electronic html)
1. One Direction (Musical group)--Juvenile literature. 2. Rock
musicians--England--Biography--Juvenile literature. 3. Boy bands--
England--Juvenile literature. I. Title.

ML3930.O66P47 2013
782.42164092'2--dc23
[B]
                                                    2013001648

Crabtree Publishing Company

Printed in the USA/052013/JA20130412

Published in Canada
Crabtree Publishing
616 Welland Ave.
St. Catharines, ON
L2M 5V6

Published in the United States
Crabtree Publishing
PMB 59051
350 Fifth Avenue, 59th Floor
New York, New York 10118

Published in the United Kingdom
Crabtree Publishing
Maritime House
Basin Road North, Hove
BN41 1WR

Published in Australia
Crabtree Publishing
3 Charles Street
Coburg North
VIC, 3058

CONTENTS

Words that are defined in the glossary are in
bold type the first time they appear in the text.

A New Direction

The story of the band One Direction, called 1D for short, is a musical Cinderella story. A few years ago, the "boys" did not even know each other. Today, they are in the hottest group in the **music industry**—worldwide!

British Beginnings

Each member of 1D grew up in the British Isles. The British Isles are made up of the United Kingdom (England, Scotland, Wales, and Northern Ireland) and Ireland.

One Direction arrives for the 2012 BRIT Awards, which are a British version of the Grammys.

What's in a Name?

Dreamed up by band member Harry Styles, the name One Direction reflects the boys' self-confidence and ambition. It announces to the world that the band is planning on heading only one way—up to the very top! The boys are now super-famous. Everything they do—especially who they date—is big news.

Harry is snapped leaving Central Park Zoo with American singer-songwriter Taylor Swift.

He Said It

Even though I'd always wanted to be in a band and sing on stage when I was growing up, I never imagined it would actually happen.
—Harry Styles, in *Dare to Dream: Life as One Direction*, 2012

Hello, Louis!

Louis William Tomlinson is the oldest member of the band. He was born on Christmas Eve, 1991, in Doncaster, South Yorkshire, England. Louis was raised in a large family with four sisters. He likes to dress sharp and loves shopping for clothes, especially striped shirts.

Natural Talents

Louis is a natural when it comes to singing. He landed roles in several of his high school's productions, including *Grease*. Before teaming up with One Direction, Louis had very little vocal training. His musical influences include British artists Robbie Williams and Ed Sheeran.

Louis takes a break from the *Up All Night* tour to go surfing at Manly Beach in Sydney, Australia.

He Said It

I've always loved [Robbie Williams]. He's just so cheeky, he can get away with anything. His performances are unbelievable.
—Louis Tomlinson, *Now Magazine*

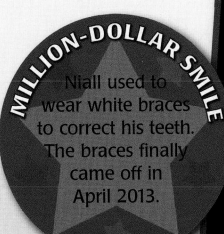

MILLION-DOLLAR SMILE

Niall used to wear white braces to correct his teeth. The braces finally came off in April 2013.

Niall struts his stuff onstage at the Apollo Theatre in London, England.

Hello, Niall!

Niall James Horan is the only Irish member in the band. He was born on September 13, 1993, in Mullingar, County Westmeath, Ireland. Niall's interest in music began in elementary school. He learned the **recorder** and sang in the choir. He began playing guitar when he was 12 years old. A year later he started singing at, and winning, local talent shows. His mother, father, and older brother were always very supportive of his musical talent. Known as "the funny one" of the group, Niall is very **sociable** and likes to meet and talk with people.

Music Man

Niall loves Irish rock band The Script, as well as Bon Jovi. He's also a fan of swing music, which is a kind of jazz. His favorite swing performers are Frank Sinatra and Michael Bublé.

7

Hello, Zayn!

Zayn Jawaad Malik calls Bradford, West Yorkshire, England his home. His birthday is January 12, 1993. Zayn comes from a close-knit family and has three sisters. He likes fashion and pays careful attention to his personal style—especially his hair! He is also talented at drawing and likes creating **caricatures** of the guys in 1D.

Talented Teen

Like Louis, Zayn was cast in his school's production of *Grease*. The teachers at his performing arts school quickly recognized his singing talents. They encouraged him to join the school choir and, later, to try out for *The X Factor*. Zayn has always loved **R&B** and rap music. Bruno Mars is one of his favorite musical artists.

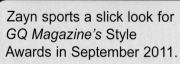

Zayn sports a slick look for *GQ Magazine's* Style Awards in September 2011.

He Said It

Life is funny. Things change, people change, but you will always be you, so stay true to yourself and never sacrifice who you are for anyone.
—Zayn Malik, Twitter, December 26, 2010

Hello, Harry!

Harry Edward Styles—the youngest member of One Direction—was born on February 1, 1994. He grew up in Holmes Chapel, Cheshire, England, with his mom, dad, and older sister Gemma. Besides being a talented singer, charming Harry is known for his self-confidence and wacky, joking ways.

Early Influences

When he was 13, Harry became the lead singer in a band called White Eskimo. The band competed in a talent show at his school and later performed at weddings and other paying **gigs**. Harry loves bands like Foster the People and Coldplay. He also likes to listen to the giants of rock 'n roll such as Elvis Presley and The Beatles.

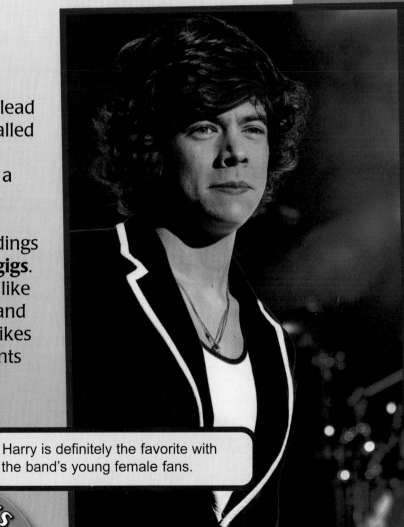

Harry is definitely the favorite with the band's young female fans.

NICKNAMES

Close friends sometimes call Harry "Hazza" or "H."

All five members of the band are singers, but Harry and Liam share the lead vocals.

Hello, Liam!

Liam James Payne was born on August 29, 1993. He has two older sisters, and he grew up in Wolverhampton, West Midlands, England. From birth, Liam has had a health issue because one of his kidneys did not work properly. Recently, however, he got the good news from his doctor that both of his kidneys are now in good working order. Liam is sometimes called "Papa Smurf," because he is the responsible one in the band.

The Jock

Liam is athletic and during his school years became a first-class long-distance runner. When he was 12, he took up boxing to defend himself against older kids who were bullying him. He joined his school choir when he was around 13 years old. His musical influences include Justin Timberlake and the band Take That.

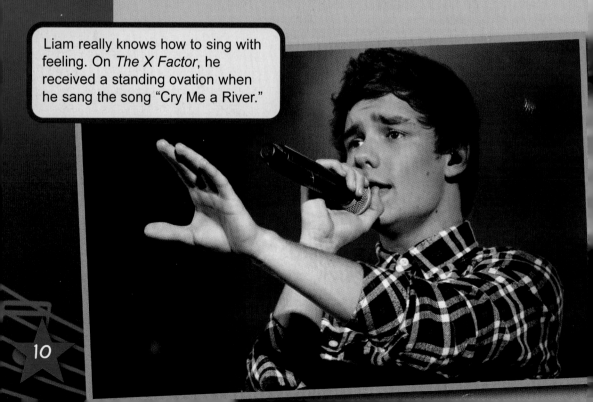

Liam really knows how to sing with feeling. On *The X Factor*, he received a standing ovation when he sang the song "Cry Me a River."

The Game Changer

In the summer of 2010, Niall, Zayn, Liam, Harry, and Louis each tried out for the British musical competition, *The X Factor* as **solo artists**. Europe's most popular talent show, *The X Factor* has been so successful that its producer, **talent scout** Simon Cowell, also created a North American version of the show.

TRY, TRY AGAIN! Louis and Liam had both (unsuccessfully) auditioned for *The X Factor* before making it in Series 7.

How It Works

Each season, the show begins with **auditions** in front of celebrity judges and an audience. The judges vote to decide who moves on to the next levels—bootcamp and the judges' houses. Celebrity singers **coach** the contestants for the final rounds, which are shown live on television and voted on by viewers. Winners of *The X Factor* receive one million pounds—that's about one-and-a-half million U.S. dollars.

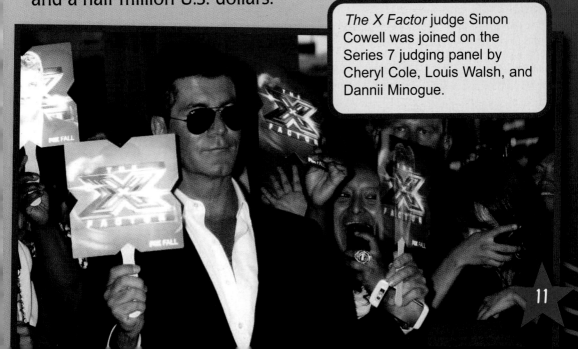

The X Factor judge Simon Cowell was joined on the Series 7 judging panel by Cheryl Cole, Louis Walsh, and Dannii Minogue.

Banding Together

Niall, Zayn, Liam, Harry, and Louis all made it to the bootcamp level as solo acts—but no further. It was guest judge Nicole Scherzinger, former lead singer of the group The Pussycat Dolls, who suggested that the boys join together to form a band. The five young singers agreed and moved on to the judges' houses, not as solo acts but as a group that had never performed together. It was time to play catch-up, and quickly! To get to know each other, the boys met at a house owned by Harry's dad to **rehearse** as the new band—One Direction.

Harry, Niall, and Louis take a break from rehearsals for *The X Factor* finals.

Mess and Tell

They say that the best way to get to know someone is to live with them. One Direction shared a room in Spain for the judges' house round, and then again in London, England at the contestants' house. They soon learned that Louis was the messiest, Zayn and Niall were the tidiest—and that Harry snored the loudest!

He Said It

I was the only one of the guys who really had to think about whether or not it was a good idea to become a band. I'd been working as a solo artist for so long that I couldn't imagine not doing that, but as soon as I made the decision to go for it I knew I'd done the right thing.
—Liam, in *Dare to Dream: Life as One Direction*, 2012

Fan Favorites

Throughout the competition, the boys were the most popular contestants. They won millions of fans with their entertaining performances. Fans started Facebook pages, dedicated YouTube videos, and took to Twitter to support 1D. Even Simon Cowell, who is known for his harsh criticism, had only good things to say about One Direction.

And *The X Factor* Winner is . . .

. . . Matt Cardle! One Direction did not win *The X Factor* competition or even come in second. In fact, they placed third. **Social media** exploded with disappointment as shocked fans raged online. Even Simon Cowell was surprised they didn't win. So, after the show, Simon called the five into his office and offered them a **recording contract** on the spot with his record label, Syco.

Simon Cowell and the band after they came third in *The X Factor*.

13

Up All Night

The next few months were a whirlwind for the new band. They worked on recording their **debut** album in Los Angeles and went on tour in the U.K. with other acts from *The X Factor*. One Direction's first album *Up All Night* is perfect pop rock, with lyrics that touch on topics such as having fun, falling in love, and being heartbroken. Different songwriters worked on the tracks, but the boys co-wrote "Taken," "Everything About You," and "Same Mistakes." In November of 2011, the album reached Number Two in the U.K. chart in its first week, becoming Britain's fastest-selling debut album ever.

POPULAR POP

One Direction were not the first to release an album called *Up All Night*. At least ten other albums of the same name have been made, including one by British band East 17.

Instant Hit

One Direction's first single, "What Makes You Beautiful," was released in September 2011, a few months before their album came out, and reached Number One in its first week. Since then, it has sold more than five million copies, making it one of the best-selling singles in history.

Louis and Harry chat on a radio station in Belfast, Northern Ireland, just before the release of "What Makes You Beautiful."

Touring Up All Night

Shortly after releasing their first single, 1D began touring to support *Up All Night*. In 2011 and 2012 they performed in Europe, Australia, and North America. As Niall noted, 1D loved connecting with their fans but the tour left them exhausted.

WHIRLWIND TOUR

The *Up All Night* tour was true to its name! Worldwide, the band performed 62 concerts in about six months.

Tour Life

The *Up All Night* tour was the longest time any of the boys had been away from home. During travel time or time off from performing, Louis said that he and the others did really normal things such as calling home, playing soccer, watching movies, and playing video games.

Fans choose from a selection of One Direction merchandise during the *Up All Night* tour.

Stateside Success

One Direction achieved something no other U.K. band had ever done before—not even The Beatles! Their first album, *Up All Night*, debuted at Number One on the *Billboard* 200, a weekly ranking of albums with the highest sales in the United States. Fans in North America were ready for a new British invasion, and they welcomed 1D with open arms . . . and lots of screaming.

Tour Highlights

During the U.S. part of the *Up All Night* tour, they found time to perform in New York City for the late night television show *SNL* (*Saturday Night Live*) with celebrity host, Sofia Vergara. Another highlight was playing the legendary Madison Square Gardens. They also visited Universal Studios in Orlando, Florida.

The "fab five" make a guest appearance on KISS FM Chicago as they tour the United States.

He Said It

*[Being compared to The Beatles] seems ridiculous to us, because they were such **icons**.*
—Harry Styles, in *The Daily Mirror*, March 16, 2012

Directioners Rock

The boys were amazed at the warm reception they got in North America. They hadn't expected to enjoy the same success there as in the U.K. and recognized that it was all due to their loyal fans. They make sure they show their gratitude by answering fans' text questions—even during concerts!

Directioners in Somersdale, New Jersey, wait for the band to arrive at a CD signing in March 2012.

He Said It

The [American] fans have just been amazing. We're not from [America] . . . so to be treated so nicely has been amazing.
—Harry Styles, on NBC5's *Backstage*, March 26, 2012

Social Media Stars

In the past, bands have taken years to reach international superstardom, but One Direction have achieved it in less than two years. Part of their immediate worldwide popularity has to do with social media such as Twitter, Facebook, and YouTube. The boys have more than six million Twitter followers and counting. They often use Twitter to share personal thoughts and experiences with fans. They even offer to follow fans online. This creates some seriously loyal fans!

Surrounded by a crush of fans, the boys perform in New York on the *Today Show* in March 2012.

He Said It

Twitter has been a major factor in getting our name out there in the States. Just as Twitter has gone up, so we have, too.
—Liam Payne, in *The Daily Mirror*, March 17, 2012

Connecting with 1D

There is an amazing online community of Directioners. Fans from around the globe have created Facebook pages, YouTube channels, fan fiction blogs, Twitter support accounts, and Tumblr pages dedicated to the boys of 1D. To provide more official information, the band's website has been designed for fans in 25 different nations.

facebook

Search for people, places and things

Find Frien

One Direction
13,829,180 likes · 723,057 talking about this

Like   Listen

Musician/Band
The new single 'One Way or Another (Teenage Kicks)' out now! http://smarturl.it/1drednoseday

About   Photos   Likes   Newsletter   Music Videos

👍 13m

Highlights ▾

Likes   See all

Savan Kotecha
Musician/Band   👍 Like

Ed Sheeran
3 friends also like this.   👍 Like

SYCO
Record Label   👍 Like

Like

ROMANCE RUMORS

1D fans love to read about who the boys are dating. They love it so much that the Internet is full of fictional stories about the boys finding love with fans!

Fans follow the boys' Facebook page to find out what the band is doing.

CLASS ACT

Before auditioning for *The X Factor*, Zayn considered himself more of an actor than a singer. Fans are glad he's sharing more of his talents now!

One Direction's first acting job as a group was on Disney's *iCarly* in January 2012. The band flew to Hollywood to record an episode of the popular Nickelodeon hit series. The episode called "iGo One Direction" **aired** on April 7, 2012, and almost four million viewers tuned in to watch!

1D pose with *iCarly* star Miranda Cosgrove during filming of the episode dedicated to them.

She Said It

It was really fun having One Direction on iCarly. I love having musical guests on the show. They sang their song, "What Makes You Beautiful." It was all of our first times meeting these guys, and they were really nice.

—Miranda Cosgrove, who plays Carly in *iCarly*, in *Life Story: One Direction 2012 Diary*

Feeling the Love

One Direction has also appeared on many televised awards shows. The boys have been thrilled to win so many awards themselves. In 2012 they won Best Single at the 2012 BRIT Awards—a dream come true. They also cleaned up at the MTV Video Music Awards in 2012. Since they grew up watching MTV, the boys said they were honored to even be at the awards.

An Epic Show

The band's biggest TV performance came in August 2012. They were invited to sing "What Makes You Beautiful" at the closing ceremonies for the 2012 London Olympics. More than 100 million viewers around the world watched.

The boys of 1D performing at the closing ceremonies for the 2012 Olympic Games in London.

Can't Get Enough

The group's first tour was turned into a concert DVD, *Up All Night—The Live Tour*. There is also a **documentary** called *The Only Way is Up* that shows tour footage, down time for the boys off stage, and the fans themselves and their reactions to 1D.

One Direction answer questions from fans in Amsterdam, The Netherlands.

He Said It

Seventeen: What's your favorite song to perform?
LT: Probably "Up All Night" because it has a certain joy. It's not really staged – we just walk slowly around the stage. The crowd responds to that song really well.
—Louis, Seventeen Magazine

Reading Up

Online stories and interviews about 1D are everywhere. The band released their official autobiography, *Dare to Dream: Life as One Direction*, in January of 2012. The book shares the boys' success story from their own personal perspectives.

One Direction **promote** their autobiography at a book signing.

BEST-SELLING AUTHORS

So many fans read *Dare to Dream* that it made it to Number One on *The New York Times* Bestsellers List! It also landed on other bestsellers lists around the world.

Giving Back

The guys in 1D are wildly successful, but they manage to stay grounded. Although they love to joke around, 1D also have a serious side. They use their fame and fortune to give back to fans and to those in need.

The guys love hosting and performing at fundraising events. In 2012, 1D were excited to sing the official single for the Children in Need Appeal Show. The show was part of an annual campaign to benefit disadvantaged children in the U.K.

In 2013 the 1D boys were asked to draw self-portraits to raise money for a youth charity called Vinspired. Fans placed bids in an online auction to win the pictures.

Personal appearances are another way 1D help raise money for those in need. Flying Start was one of the more memorable appearances – it had 1D taking fans on a charity airplane flight. The guys also meet with sick fans as part of hospice visits. The Rays of Sunshine foundation has worked with 1D to lift the spirits of many fans.

Inspiring Fans

The guys also take time to lend a hand with Greenpeace and the U.K. Comic Relief organization.
In 2013, Niall and Harry visited Ghana with Comic Relief and took to Twitter to tell their fans about their experiences. Niall shared what he learned about the extent of poverty and urged fans to get involved to help fundraising.

1D recorded the official song for Red Nose Day 2013 called *One Way or Another (Teenage Kicks)*. All sales from the single go to charity.

He Said It

Massive thanks to @rednoseday for taking us to Ghana! It was incredible! real eye opener! We take so much for granted over here!
—Niall, on Twitter, January 15, 2013

The Next Big Move

Enthusiastic 1D fans eagerly awaited the November 2012 release of the band's second album *Take Me Home*. Its cover shows the boys climbing all over a red telephone booth.

No Place Like Home

The band came up with the title for *Take Me Home* together. In an interview, Niall admitted that he and the others loved traveling around the world but—as Dorothy says in *The Wizard of Oz*—really "there's no place like home."

The boys emerge from a London recording studio during the making of *Take Me Home*.

He Said It

[Take Me Home] is not too different from the first [album] . . . We're obviously nervous—the second album—you never know what you're going to get from it. We're really excited about it. It's really heavy on guitars and drums.
—Niall, on KISS-FM, August 30, 2012

Single Success

The first single off *Take Me Home*, "Live While We're Young," reached Number One so quickly, it broke the record for the fastest-selling single in the U.S. by a non-American band.

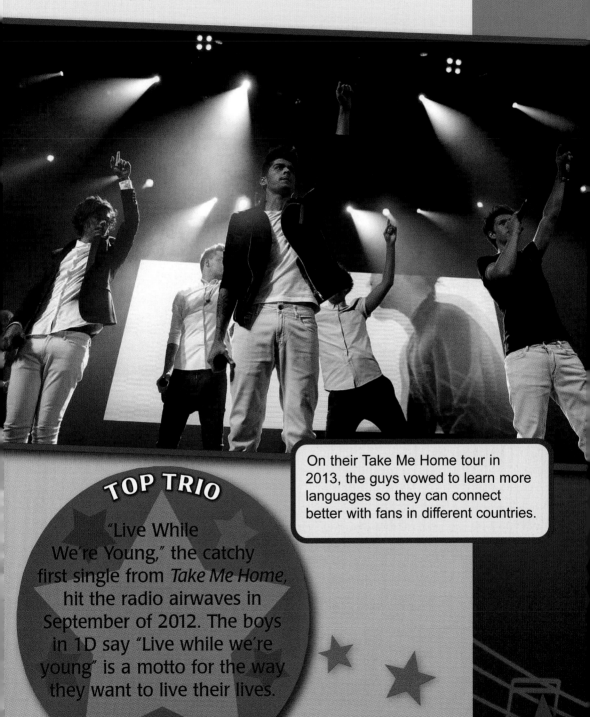

On their Take Me Home tour in 2013, the guys vowed to learn more languages so they can connect better with fans in different countries.

TOP TRIO

"Live While We're Young," the catchy first single from *Take Me Home*, hit the radio airwaves in September of 2012. The boys in 1D say "Live while we're young" is a motto for the way they want to live their lives.

Big Business

One Direction is now so famous that the toymaker Hasbro has produced fashionably dressed action figures of the boys. They are also the stars of an upcoming graphic novel, *Fame: One Direction*.

A page from *Fame: One Direction*, the graphic novel that tells the story of the boy band from their start on *The X Factor*.

Next Direction?

Despite the album's name, *Take Me Home* actually takes the boys away once more. Barely stopping to catch their breath, they hit the road again early in 2013 to promote the new album. 1D will also be in 3D soon. The tour is being filmed and will once again feature the boys in concert and backstage.

Niall was quoted as saying that 1D want to follow in the path of the group Take That, a **boy band** that re-formed after ten years apart to record a more mature album. With their latest album, Louis says that 1D have improved vocally and that their experience and growing friendship has made them a better band. There really is only one direction for this band—UP!

Timeline

1991: Louis William Tomlinson is born on December 24.

1993: Zayn Jawaad Malik is born on January 12.
Liam James Payne is born on August 29.
Niall James Horan is born on September 13.

1994: Harry Edward Styles is born on February 1.

2010: Niall, Zayn, Liam, Louis, and Harry each audition as solo artists for *The X Factor*.

2010: One Direction forms as a band on *The X Factor* and finishes in third place.

2011: "What Makes You Beautiful" hits #1 in the U.K. chart in its first week.

2011: 1D releases their debut album, *Up All Night*, in the U.K. and begins their *Up All Night* tour.

2012: "What Makes You Beautiful" is released in North America.

2012: *Up All Night* becomes the first U.K. album to hit #1 on the *Billboard* chart in its first week.

2012: 1D appears in their first acting job on *iCarly*.

2012: 1D performs in the 2012 London Olympics closing ceremony.

2012: 1D wins a BRIT Award and three MTV Video Music Awards.

2012: *Take Me Home* is released in November in the U.K. and North America and reaches #1 in the U.S.

2013: 1D begins their *Take Me Home* world tour.

Glossary

aired When a program is first shown on TV

audition When a singer or actor tries out for a job or part by giving a short performance

boy band A pop group of young male singers who are usually still teenagers

caricatures Drawings that exaggerate physical characteristics of the subject in a comical manner

coach To give training and encouragement

debut First

documentary A film that charts the history of a person, place, or thing

gig A performance or concert put on in return for money

icon Something or someone that is admired greatly

music industry All the businesses and people who are involved in making and selling music

promote To do things that will help a product sell more—for example, a band usually goes on tour to promote an album

R&B Rhythm and blues, a form of popular African American music

recorder A simple, flute-like musical instrument

recording contract A legal agreement in which a company known as a record label commits to producing an artist's music

rehearse To practice

sociable Friendly and able to talk with confidence to others

social media Ways in which people communicate with each other using the Internet

solo artist A performer who appears on his or her own, rather than in a group

talent scout Someone whose job is to find new acts or performers

Find Out More

Books

Boone, Mary. *One Direction: What Makes You Beautiful*
Triumph Books, 2012.

Raso, Anne. *One Direction.* Andrews McMeel
Publishing, 2012.

Troy, Michael. *Fame: One Direction*
Bluewater Productions, 2012.

One Direction. *Dare to Dream, Life as One Direction*
Harper Collins, 2012

DVDs

One Direction: Up All Night–The Live Tour (U.S. Version)
Columbia, 2012

One Direction: The Only Way is Up
Entertainment One, 2012

Websites

One Direction Music
www.onedirectionmusic.com
The band's official website

Twitter

@onedirection, @Louis_Tomlinson, @Harry_Styles,
@Real_Liam_Payne, @NiallOfficial, @Zaynmalik

Facebook

https://www.facebook.com/onedirectionmusic

YouTube

http://www.youtube.com/user/onedirectionchannel

Index

About the Author

Lynn Peppas is an author of more than 60 children's non-fiction books and the mother of five children. She has worked in the publishing industry as a freelance author and editor for over a dozen years. When not reading or writing she enjoys cooking, biking, and nature hikes.